Copyright © 2018 by Jay Passer
Cover Art: Rhea Adri
Layout: Pski's Porch

All rights reserved. No part of this book may be reproduced in any form by any electronic or mechanical means including photocopying, recording, or information storage and retrieval without permission in writing from the author.

ISBN-13: 978-0998847689
ISBN-10: 0998847682
for more books, visit Pski's Porch:
www.pskisporch.com

Printed in U.S.A.

They Lied To Me When They Said Everything Would Be Alright

By Jay Passer

Contents

my afterlife   1
independence day   2
to do list   3
the milk years   4
dictator of jazz   5
banned in the cafes of paris   6
the crush   7
one poet per billionaire   8
punk tutorial 9
obsolete as the radio is bleak   10
self in blue   11
the domestic front   12
one last   13
the man from pompeii   14
marco polo   15
gentrified   16
closure in 3-point perspective   17
anonymous   18
xmas or bust 19
from the abstract to the concrete 20
ghat astrology   21
booked for the next incarnation   22
binary moan   23
reversal of fortune   25
the origin of subtitles   26
pocketbook martyr   27
the felines   28
what we're supposed to do 30
one for nothing   31
chinatown   32

tenderloin blues 33
why don't we 34
some bookmarks 36
recipe for caliban 37
trap door to nowhere 38
pingpong jellyroll 39
we were kids no more 42
remember when 43
the which doctor 44
the black hole 45
even goodbyes have given up 46
big city 47
against the urge to finish 48
if you'll let me love you 49
brothers 50
the blame 58
bilingual 59
leah 60
quarantine 62
drawing from life 63
not a morning person 64
it had to be the accent 65
shape of a bullet headed home 66
let's go camping, she said 67
the hermit of the inner sunset 68
north beach black and blue 69
perfect states of innocence 71
how's it feel to want 72
i liked it better when you were a junkie 73
the legacy 75
hollywood 76
the short term 77

no hand in the naming   78
fish   79
a moment of introspection 80
hotel modigliani   81
shell shock   83
romance   84
blackjack   85
the gospel according to acid pete 87
they may very well turn against me   93
how to go hungry when revoked of dreams   95
modern art   96
my way   97
war   100
nowadays   101
history   102
middle east of complacency   103
old men clutching   104
power out(r)age   106
missy 107

my afterlife

I walked into the new
Cafe and found a booth.

The waitress wore a garter
Belt and thong.

I'll take the crow's egg omelet
And coyote hash.

She tattooed my order
Upon the skin of her inner
Thigh.

I think I like
This place.

independence day

in the old country, say it, old country

we barbecue lesser icons
on planks of wood

black salmon, ivory red
ambergris in bottle

it's a nice day outside, say
nice day

time to scorch the dead at premium
holler and whoop

belly full, is not America the rule?

to do list

Look for a new place to live on Craigslist
Shave face and manicure eyebrows
Kali's in town
Go see Chumpy Joe about theater piece
Call the old man in his decrepitude and senility
Football scores to argue and digress
Upon the morality of multi-million $ defensive lines
Fabricate for edibility the cantaloupe crying for attention on the dresser
Fragrant orb found treasured in Chinatown
Perched on a garbage receptacle
Cut off feet and cauterize with log embers from beach bonfire
Seal Beach
Ocean Beach
North Beach
You know the beach as far as a promised Paradise
There are things to attend to
For sure
Through the karma and manifest destiny shit
Stagger a bit before hitting the pavement
Forget laundry.

the milk years

I turned 12 years old
amidst some controversy
they found out what I was allergic to

the stepmother sat me down at the kitchen
table
and ran down the list:

the dog
dust
pollen from the acacia tree out back
milk

they bought a hair brush for the collie
Lemon Pledge for the
furniture
but if my father ever swung an ax
I certainly missed
that part

I never picked the
crunch berries
out of Cap'n Crunch again

the good news is I only have
3 cavities
at the age of 49

dictator of jazz

I am a drill bit in the jaw of a crocodile
A lottery check winner in triplicate
I'm waiting for the sign from the casket maker
The flag slaps against the battleship gray of my solitude
Sparks fly in the wake of midnight nightmare visions
Skulking brim pulled low against my specs I hit Washington Square
Pop over to Stockton for a pinched apple as the Buddha glares
I'm traipsing through the Broadway Tunnel happily fumigated
With tax-paying law-abiding poison melee of exhaust
I am paprika on the proboscis of a dragonfly
Cracked ribs shoulders of granite and intrinsic arteries
Mimic of the City a creeping crippled crow
Drink of paralysis shot of defibrillation crack of starlight
And the yawning omniscient entirety of nowhere left to go
As the sand-blown decaying walls out by Ocean Beach
Hem in the Pacific Rim a Colossus there's no escape from
I am a butte on the spine of the Sierras
A saxophone bottled with inverse propaganda
Dictator of Jazz wooing oceans
And girls with seaweed cut short behind the ears

banned in the cafes of paris

they got me cold,
cuffed to the bumper of a prowler bound for the clink
in the nanosecond it takes to order chile verde
at Zorro's.

hop to it, debark South Van Ness, check out the mamacitas
clicking in black pumps over the blue tiles,
aroma descent from hotel window pretty putrid please.

I chucked the gold to the curb in time for rivulets of fog
to congeal within tap tap the vein, coffee table the last frame
in a conscious blend,
spike of formica, death's head futility on the dime.

they got me on ice, space
between planets, they had to call in
for translation.

window dressing of the silent film, musculature of mannequins,
faux painted Gucci denim graces jutting assets,
I slap past donut shop, the pun attracting flies.

Mission Street, plantain peels squashed to gutter curb,
mortgage for ammoniac cardboard shanty
the pay-off of shopping-cart possessors,
litter of dreams on long consignment.

I got 60 days to think about it
swathed in County blues
mismatched plastic sandals, armed with tiny lottery
pencil.

the crush

I love you Lindsey Lohan
your milk white body and galaxy of freckles
your deep rich voice
your crazy glitter eyes
your various addictions
the media wants to cure you because the media
is a barnyard animal demanding conformity
of all wild beasts
women despise you while secretly coveting your hotness
wishing
through their warped patina of morality
they had your tits
and ass and
notoriety
men pretend to disdain you in front of their
indignant wives and girlfriends
while later imagining your pursed bitch lips as they
prematurely ejaculate
I love you LiLo
your scandals and recklessness
your on-set shenanigans
your mug shots
your flirty whorish outfits
your brazen manipulation of the judicial system
even
your passé portrayal of Elizabeth Taylor
whose first screen kiss
was shared with a horse

one poet per billionaire

Would solve the problem
Set up a sweatshop in a tree house
Serve coffee in one of 32K locations worldwide
Serve McFalafel to Hezbollah
The played-out woes shallowly buried in moon dust
Taxes ferreted out of munitions manufacturers
Laughter per price point versus prescribed depressant allowance
Advertisements for chocolate syrup spandex
Lysergic acid paint ball
Sports that justify ritual assassination
One poet per billionaire would solve all the world's problems

punk tutorial

man am I ever hooked up
hooked in
persevering

got a grade A+
in fuck up
what landed me here

was a forest fire
put out
with canned beer

obsolete as the radio is bleak

All the jazz settings
All the fedoras
The emergency calls to the fire department
Televised rescue scenarios
Soundtracks of catcalls for taxicabs
The double-decker bus set to third-world imbroglio
How to chop off a chicken's head with aplomb
While balancing cell phones from fingertip to ear
Cybernetic showgirls strut and advertise
Timpani set to porn on the fly
To the power of ten fingering the spine
Where motive begins captured in the telescopic lens
Session musician incapacitated
The smooth child sitting before a roomful of eyes
Cigarette plumes and rocks glass in hand
All the black-and-white sirens
The still-life alibis
All the established outtakes of couture
The boots and fancy oyster shell specs
Inimitable street-life flashing the price
How to forge the ticket
One win away from
I'm out of here

self in blue

alive despite torture device
man with options for hire
rewind news feed

super victim
with baccalaureate in
opiated weaponry

thoughts scripted for distortion
open heart carved from
treasure chest

mirror shard reflecting
sacral svadhisthana
some beer bellied bespectacle

four seam fastball for a brain
wolf in need of a
shave

the domestic front

we're casting feathers
on Election Day.

in the
inner breast pocket
of the Incumbent's flawless black tux
there's a well-placed baggie
of pure white shit

Lincoln Bedroom,
no blame.

seagull
      egret
           owl
eagle

crow's heart beat of hope
how best to christen fleet warships
Goddess notwithstanding.

backyard tree-house shoebox stash
satellite nano-tech minutiae of quarks
staging ground for
encrypted albumen

sum golden egg
torture cell echoes embalmed in cinder block

Air Force One
over duck pond.

one last

tragedy benign
facing a camera or mirror

somebody's trying to dream here

two blackbirds along the curb
pecking at specks of the moon

volcanic tectonic

one last, to dispel the bile of anxiety
rising in throat, the fragility of ribcage
flitting with the ghosts of sparrows

quit staring at that screen!

limbs, particles of the earth's hub
centrifugal spokes illuminating whale song
silver strands mercurial, larvae radioactive
crickets in unison with ancient archetypes

bombs away, boys!

wish list monotony
the lottery of sparkling rain

I want to disbelieve in horses
corpses the
felony of words

the man from pompeii

He came up with the theory
That in actuality
Humanity is a race of slave labor
From another planet

Instead of being abducted
Taken elsewhere
And experimented upon
It's really

Us
Alien to the Earth
Which makes perfect sense
When you think about the fact

Insects have
Humanity outnumbered
By billions
In weight alone

I haven't run the numbers
By my attorney
But it's a decent guess
It won't be long

marco polo

I am the conduit between a horse and God
I take the bus between my stomach and yours
Your scent bottled and sold for a thousand miles an hour
Straight from the stables you sit for a spell
I feast on the scent of Cassiopeia in your navel
Following a sure path from the gas pump to the oasis
I am a contemplative beast before the slaughter
Vegetable remains distributed amidst bovine nomenclature
Spleen rises in the esophagus of supernova
I am dire research accomplished in the bowels of the Earth
I notate the variables and ascertain the inconsistencies
I rise like a gas or magma or volleys of light
I am ore in the vein of an unexplored expedition
Take a minute for siesta on our way to the corral
Mount me sure and steady and try not to spook me
Try not to traverse the heavens only to wake up in chains
A hint of cinnamon a dash of cardamom a tincture of opium
Hidden under the saddle your works mingle with mine
Our blood mingles under Orion and the ocean wide
We climax in time for the season finale
Curtains on opus operandi

gentrified

first the lethal drummer across the hall
then the next door yoga girl with such curly red hair

systematically replaced with robotic urbanites
a pain and panic twitch inside while the doors rattle

they're moving in!
well-oiled laughter, secret mechanical lives

a betrayal of my well-kept silences
inevitable lonesome blues intuit

a brisk knock on early morning door,
notarized invitation for

perhaps a nice hot cup of
eviction

closure in 3-point perspective

day by day we wait
for what

by strident daylight monotony
or some moon demanding anticlimax

sick and wasting hours between
servitude and excess

brawls about the city
strewn with

clacking and pop
of operatic gaiety

say we
won the World Series

slivers not lost
on the thumb of the maker

dynasties lacking the mistrial
of dire awakening

hungover
or not at all

anonymous

it used to be I'd sit
in the back row of the middle-school classroom

banks of fluorescent light where the sky wasn't
I stared at my shoes and just managed a passing grade

now I can't depend on centralized heat
since the account's gone to collection

I siphon my whiskey from holes in the walls
what I've learned could wallpaper a matchbox

yet all I really lack is a map of the universe
and a fishing permit

xmas or bust

landed in Sacramento
straight off Amtrak
the year Mayan
from the confines of a shoebox orbiting the moon
brain function close to nil
the New Year impractical
dwarf maple canopy performing umbrella for prone alligator
rolling back my eyes to the history of molten origin
the sparkling reveal of the saw blade perforating
winter skies

from the abstract to the concrete

a drink at the fountain
toss in a quarter
not worth much
make it a gold tooth.

check your messages
check your pulse.

I don't mind the idea of dying
my family would whine
for a short period
then gently reflect
upon my more or less
decent traits:

"He liked cats, but was allergic to them."

ghat astrology

a void of, a bowl of,
comic book psychosis
day dream carnival mirror Cyclops
oatmeal steeped in Stolichnaya
We waited months for the mail
stuffed with mud and broken glass,
swordfights with bamboo poles
fix-it version of projected identities
replaced with a character constructed
of paper mache and hard candy
addicts of the inferno
We waited hours for phone calls
cosmic cynic, he who forged keys
some diamond encrusted holy fool
black rice, beach of stars
We slid down barrios
on sheets of acrylic for kicks
land mines like asteroids

booked for the next incarnation

Hairline gone the way of obsolete things
Body shaping up for the park bench
Wing tips replacing skateboard skids
Vivaldi rather than the Velvets
Awake to dawn of prehistoric sunrise
I've known trees with better plans than mine

binary moan

It isn't really hard, what passes for Living

your banal televised cartoons
fighting the ceiling with Jellyroll and three-fingered
fugues

I have my couch and nasty conscious imagination

The leaves quivering with the wind are a tease
Down the street at the bakery the girl who works there

She's tall and lithe, cool and young
Myself a bit blithe and dumb

Like her dad, an old oak ponderous beside the window

That which rolls
That which blows

Ode to Al Jarry
Feet painted green or face painted gold

head carved from absinthe

gold blown off the snow covered mountain
golden-paved smut-ugly streets

The smutty deaths of cars
How we fall to the muscle of the music:

rain and tire-squeal and quiet, as long as you're passed out as respectful as the normalized ape, gorilla or trained monkey

Ode to the spider, the fly!

I love the little quiet insects
the ladybug and the earwig

I listen to Jazz music while in abhorrence of the bent backache of longing,
I ignore the bitter dread of losers sulking and limping away

I research the box scores
Oh, the columns of Defeated!

myself, still awake
Deadened to the physical strenuous mortification of BEING

My birth perpetually one week from today

reversal of fortune

health is for animals
the food chain halts
with advanced
intelligence and addiction to electronics.

the arboreal world
enhanced with whittling of arias,
tsunami of symphony
does not need us to breathe.

they say dolphins evolved from land
to the seas.

why do what the next guy can do
for you.

the origin of subtitles

oh the mad numbers
the stomach of being like a bear trap in the snow
the false visas and passports of agents provocateurs
pockets sewn up, hands cuffed, led away by jerk-off cops,
locked up, forgotten
on the body itself curling up in defense
of a mightily impractical natural environment
the age of the wind the conscience of the tree
a vile pity emblematic of the false at heart

calamity time!
you better add celery salt to the crust of bread soup
we're on the cusp of not-so-greatness
the heart beat pounds for more, for indiscreet supplication
to be removed from the quarry of quintessential sculpturing,
fault-line implicit in the stone
and dog-tired of French films in the after hours
festooned in the noir of nothingness,
smoke piled loosely around the Venus of the minute's bare
white shoulders, wraith, espresso absentee

pocketbook martyr

wandering glibly across
the water of the well
I might've been mistaken
for a malarial mosquito

H20 these days
purified in France or Calistoga
natural as a malignant tumor
with power of attorney

the difference being
the firefly and sequoia
molten earth core and Mars
fear of rhyming

the felines

a couple women
amidst echoes and shadows
take off their pumps
before fighting.

I just need a bottle of water
coconut juice
and some sleep.

at the corner bodega,
a woman in line ahead of me
requests a pack of Parliaments and a
small Bic lighter
which she flicks
              flicks
                    flicks
to make sure it works.

she's high on cocaine
being it's one-thirty in the morning
she's high on meth
she's high on
life.

she is bustling with news of the cat fight
these sluts in the night street!
the Muslim behind the counter
sees it all the time
broadly he smiles
              smiles
                    smiles
he can't afford to lose a
sale.

it's another night on Broadway
the strip clubs and
pizza parlors
the bleating and screams
the night sky expanding
with dawn approaching
the constellations bright with stripper heels and
ripped spandex.

plunked in the Bay
the hard-line bridge faces the
City
with battleship hues
while the day yet to arrive
hosts rainbows and squalls
of traffic, sirens, and typical emotion -
felines we are
with the shelf life of insects
sufficient in our envy and ego
to manufacture the very
stars in the sky
and thus accomplice ourselves
in league

with ultimate promenades of history
black-and-white newsreels
the world at a standstill
the lonely
kitten
mewling at the broken
milk-bottle
another alleyway
another universe.

ooh
    la la.

what we're supposed to do

Union Square
Macy's
I stole a bunch of clothes in my mind
Accompanied by a young princess equally fiendish
Threadbare running free hand in hand laughing
We nestled in the tall grass at the park at Embarcadero
There were statues and circus animals and people acting chaste like stalled traffic
Buses on the murderous route assailing the sky blue
Tunnels gray black and cobalt moons and terrific tunes
We sobbed and smiled full fed enfeebled with triumphant spirituality
The dream new to the mind and bones
Stretched out in the hotel room
All the insects of the world submerged
The bay the ferries running the bridges the sky
God the poetry of your smile singing silently as we kiss
We are made to love and yet take our sweet time
Myself
Alone
Tonight spine bent hair graying and big veined feet
Pining with old songs and cheap spirits
Wishing for you demanding of the cosmos
Wryly unwilling to accept our nights of music numbering once a week
Days followed by wolves panting with impossible hunger

one for nothing

hard on listen to your hero
microphone mezzanine
electric ceiling got a fizzy
trained for sleaze

go God get me another wad
tickle the recession the back jean pocket
I was born between the pages of a
National Geographic
in psych ward #2

dim the fan and jerk the caffeine
swim to severing finger beings
a satisfied smear grimacing
passionate art students punch

lottery or ballot box

chinatown

We pressed against the moonlit doorway
She gave herself so freely I thought I might
Fuck her right then and there in strobes of urban alacrity.

Of course I have a small bit of integrity left
In this calloused soul of a body
I walked her to her car.

There's nothing like the lights of Chinatown late at night
Everyone has closed up shop and the neon's not unlike
Alien stars carousing.

Her small mouth fit mine
Like a perfected dose of heroin
Once a person has recovered from humanity.

Is it too early to discuss
Love?
I struggle to see eye to eye with sleeplessness.

tenderloin blues

I am addict
of small rooms
lots of loud noise
I can't prevent
and pornography
in my head
not bodies per se
but oil percolating
running slim
beneath the ground
I am sound as I notice
the dubious air
sneaking features a floor above
somebody the son or daughter
of another
motherfucker
plots and plans the demise
of my conscious
insignificance
it is no small rule
a blue pint bottle
a little whitewashed fool
girl reckoning womanhood
demon asthmatic hands amidst
clouds ponying up for pollution status
I am big feet
gray hair and brain
need shampoo
a break from logic and opera
industrial streets
refrain

why don't we

why don't we
recall the poignancy of wartime

perished along the dust of the road
serpentine prey of molecular memory

somebody gasped a last breath
chewing an ice cream
grenade

literature antiquated algebraic
electron at the tip of the bayonet

pretty passing
saints hung from steaming toadstools

one lost peon draped with a flag died the day
after tomorrow

he fell off a barstool
toasting a friend
met his maker in throes
of carousing
just off Turk and Jones

while she
homing in submariner Mom
Sapphic
Cleopatric
or otherwise infamous
reducing the news of the fall of the sun in the sky

to
tears and voices indelibly inaudible through voids
of omniscient absence

names
dates
prophesies
laughter of a floater underwater

see if it don't
hail on saints and fools
fireflies bent on
vengeance

some bookmarks

there is bay leaf, lottery ticket
snapshot of the dog as a little pup
grocery list found in the shopping cart
matchbook from the bar down the street
memory of snow flake
rose bud from mother's grave
lock of hair from love gone cold
sliver of moon lost in space
crow's feather, bus transfer
fortune cookie's lucky number
ticket stub from multiplex, prescription cancelled
note to self demanding apology

recipe for caliban

My chocolate is cerebral beef
Bled out on the marbled planetoid surface
The interior of the death head's skull
Photographs of the landscape include
Inarticulate phosphorescent beastliness
Pinpoint radiology of cancerous joy
I read the entrails of old machine parts
Rusting by the side of the Interstate
Parts machined from organic resources
Culled from loose-leaf minutiae
Jargon of encyclopedic texts
Where I slumber amidst illegally parked halos
Celestially handicapped zones
My workforce furred of heart and rabbit-eared
The mantra of the new world being:
I put ego into the churn which develops
Considerable advances in plate tectonics

trap door to nowhere

Hidden in the recesses of astringency
There were elves and horse thieves
And tattooed limbs hanging from the trees
I took a seat among the jailed and condemned
And listened for the sermon of the damned
As the insects grew to gigantic proportions
Like in some B-movie from way back in the day
Cocktail hour on the hour
Smoking permitted everywhere
And smiles at the end of the night graced with sweet lechery

pingpong jellyroll

I escaped the crib
the heat of my mother
and a couple brushes with men
head full of badges and ammo
when she dangled
the cherry in front of my
face

look it, she goes, coy and
tipping her head and
saucy like she
does, look it what I got for you while
you were away

it was this tiny pewter statue of
Ganesh,
the Remover of Obstacles.

what does it do, I tried to
plug it in, or eat it, and
she's all
C'mon, let's go to the bar,
let's get some pizza and
hit Pete's for some
shit

done in again, railroaded, I let
her take me down
below the belt,
her creamy hands leading
eyelashes batted and where's the

cliff edge this time, for
fuck sakes.

you look hungry, let's
follow Ganesh, and That's an order, she
said
as I quite gently
removed her leopard skin spiked heel
from my ear canal
to the tune of
Sheena is a Punk

it's Taco Tuesday at the Bit Saloon,
we can play ping pong, and Pete's sure to make
an appearance.

I let her win the
war game
on the warped table, new
as I was to the fetid gloom
of freedom

disproportionately obscured by smoke
I'm invited for a session
the lady's stall, crammed
with her
fleshy thighs and Rhonda watching from the sink,
jealous as a salivating
mouth.

You'll get yours, honey pie, she purrs,
lapping at the nearly
spent bindle -
Pete gives it good, what I

heard

I get the picture. the walls be bopped, papered
with posters devising calendars
brazen with sleaze

nothing's free
on Taco Tuesday.

we were kids no more

I walk around
there's a sun out
and sirens in the street
because a kid got shot
and over there what's that
they're chopping down a 300-year-old oak tree
cool
more room to roller skate
on top of the spilled brains of the blown away kid
what street am I on
oh shit it's just another American street
Central Valley Central District South Central
they cut down all the trees in Central Park
they cut down the sun from the sky
feed us marshmallows from wicker baskets
hook us like fish and bait us with ass licks
it's fun when you think about it
especially with a good script from the psych doctor
shoot me in the temple with extract of apple pie
switch on the mobile satellite
how many hits does it take to get to the center of the website
the mirror says it's your birthday today
subtract another candle from the cake
way to celebrate
in the future your brains will resemble scrambled eggs
a fine and beautiful mess not unlike
the tree house where you first jerked off
the parking lot where they found you shot in the head
the whole solar system at the edge of its seat
the universe in fact wants its money back
I walk around with the sound turned down
with my eyes closed
it takes practice

remember when

the post office was painted in the Spanish Mission style
mural size up above the windows,
the bear up on hind legs, the bull pawing the dust
ready for battle in the ageless spectacle men
pursue to their dying gasps,
and I walked
in to purchase stamps, to stand there
dreaming of post-mortem America
where in the rancid quiet so Western and apocalyptic
I could smile big, knowing how to
light a fire without matches,
which grubs
and what bark to eat, and being so used to sleeping on floors
never achieving Social Security
sounded like
a god damned vacation.

I remember when I sat on the ground at the bus station
ticket to Tacoma in my pocket, waiting again
for the coach, waylaid and stifled trash culture
peering unabashed at my shamble to the seats in the back,
piss smell of the latrine in good company, sloshing
with the undulation of the ride
north,
and in the delirium of youthful impotence
I drank from a flask, smoked Camels in the last seat
to the rear,
waiting as if perched on a fence post, for sunset,
a black bull, a holocaust, something,
something
to take me forward to that vaunted place
I always wanted to see

the which doctor

I got my
honorary doctorate
the hard way

buried shekels and yen
underground

grew me
a cash tree
hacked that sucker down

hatched words
at the laboratory

like sparrows
minnows
cobras

fleas

the black hole

What is extraordinary
Is the ferocity
Of the slightest
Intangibility

A pinhole in your heart
What fits through
Like a tracheotomy

At the cafe
At the last dead oasis
Before the desert plain
A sinkhole in the moon
Deep space
What is exemplary
Is how to fool
Naivety squared
Prize-winning dupe
A generous helping, or two
Try shoving that through

The pinhole in your heart

even goodbyes have given up

the trees are sick of it
the animals are pissed
the land swallows bile
the sky darkens like a slapped face
birds quit singing
volcanoes bow to mere holes in the ground
baseball players sleep till one in the afternoon
priests run after whores
whores run to church
churches surf the net for poltergeists
oceans spit mermaids up onto the beaches
candy canes turn black on Christmas Day
flowers sweat like crack-heads
down on the corner fiending
pregnant with shark litters
stars cancel their cable providers
blink off one by one
until the constellations resemble not Gods of Myth
but chances missed
it's the New World
take a seat
Ma'am and Mister
even goodbyes have given up
on train platforms and kissing cousins

big city

look at the sights
bright standing tall and wow,
spandex, pierced libido on the fly

flu in the ear, cancer in the lobe
she gave it up at the base of the skyscraper
it was dark and swear to God nobody was looking.

back alley concourse, ammoniac
men and women crouching in the war zone,
neglect vs. compromise

grimy upturned faces, kind Sir?
just a dollar'll fix me up
for sure.

no buses sidles along this back street,
no taxi or EMT -
we are all going to die.

gimme purple-ridden skyline
shoes bitten with tragedy, ridden purple horizons
gimme strip coup militia of treeless boulevards.

big city mime, black and white wail the sirens.
fog interposes just like History
obscuring puppeteers.

against the urge to finish

About magic and the rifle to the ear
Mosquito hawks trained to circumnavigate the cabin
Coughing in code

Upwind the aroma of Swisher Sweet and propane
Train whistle at 5 a.m.
Dogs hoarse with unchecked validation

The magic is changing skin to meet your maker
The tree stump rotted out with insect intelligentsia
Drawl of the sun-baked picnic table

Bats on the take consider their options
Sequoia falls victim to unscrupulous
Chainsaw

Men scamper
Fatigued with feral instinct
Forgetting the words to odes to their grandmothers

if you'll let me love you

I'll whip up a hurricane
and set the house down in Rio
I will make everything electric
even the dogs and flowers
I'll abolish politics and it won't cost money
to eat at the fast-food places
because I'll burn down the fast-food places
and I'll burn the money too
I'll squirt venom from vipers into the Vatican
graffiti the Last Supper and whitewash the Sistine
I will hang myself from a rope lassoed to the moon
if you'll let me love you

brothers

her name's Asia
she strips at the Deja Vu
my brother is obsessed with her
now I see why
long and lean,
finely formed
with a wide mouth and dancing green eyes
and a jaunty jut and strut on the stage
acrobat on the pole
every man in the place salivating
in the disco ball-speckled darkness
I pull my old stingy-brim
lower over my eyes
if my girl knew where I was
she would assassinate me

Asia gyrates a last time with a coy smile
heads into the back as
Motorhead's *Ace of Spades*
fades to black
Vinnie is obviously agitated
I order a couple vodka sodas
and walk over
damn Teddy, where'd you come from?
quit sneakin' up on me!
I smile and hand Vinnie his drink
so now I'm stalking you?
well at any rate it's
good timing bro, can you spare 20 bucks?
when can't I?
I guess never

I look toward the stage
so that's Asia
yeah, that's her
Vinnie starts to light up
he gets that way, gesticulates in crazy arcs
his eyes blazing rebellion
his psyche demanding revolution
I got a good feeling about Asia
he sings
she's a goddess disguised as a strumpet
my brother the dichotomist
what're you gonna do, use her as a model?
I'm working on it
but she's not too keen about it
she thinks painting
is obsolete
she wants to star in a porn flick
well she's got a point
painting may be lucrative for the painter
but the star will always circumnavigate the cosmos
oh thanks for that, brother
how very encouraging
how 'bout that Jefferson?

a couple days later
I get an email
it's from Vinnie
describing the color of mustard in a pale sunset
as unsettling and vulgar
the faulty mechanism of cobalt
blue worse than the black and blues
entertaining suicide on the face
of a maudlin drunk
why don't you just text me bro

if you want to talk
but my brother is possessed
with Asia
and sunshine and broken buildings
squealing, jerky buses burdened with
the working class
and the squalid streets
and the faces
all the faces of the wretched and destitute
the bodies lying prone across sewer grates
steaming with the productivity of industry
meet you at the Deja Vu
being the daily mantra
the last several paintings
shocking the common public
those with no problem serving
shit sandwiches to the wedding party

I can't complain
my own girl keeps me in line
it's Valentine's Day daily with my girl
plus she's planning on
pregnancy
Vinnie tries to hide it
but he's jealous
even while I fork over cash for supplies

Asia I hope
Asia I dream
Asia I freeze
Asia I objectify
Asia I sigh

nothing to lose sleep over, right?
there's gonna be a day I choke to death

looking after your best interests, bro
I thought
but couldn't bring myself
to say

she sure looks hot up there though
straddling that pole
maybe a condescending moment
ensues
but dawn awakens, 6 AM
and down the street at Vesuvio's
the bartender hasn't even brewed the coffee yet

Asia
her eyes leaking emerald ink
saves the entire existence of humanity
with a swift smile
and spandex cross-legged
we huddle together on the second floor
looking out over the cold bustle of
Columbus
but I'm the third wheel so I
down my shooter
as my cell vibrates
gotta take off, duty calls
Vinnie perks an ear
under that jaunty Panama hat
sell something will ya?
preferably of mine?
Asia devilish
swirling her fruity vodka

the image of her
as I let myself into the gallery
projected on the future of my life

in 3-D
not a good day for happy commerce
they're betting under
while my brother
being the best painter of the bunch
is dissented and obfuscated
maybe it's the Panama hat
from that stint in Mexico City
the corn cob pipe
you know he scents his skank with lavender?
some funky rebel
most of my quiver shoots straight
it's nothing to lose your cool over
but then there's my
brother
he causes me endless torment
genius is like that
I get on the line to the Hague
to Prague
an important lady in Philadelphia
places like Los Angeles, Melbourne
Tel Aviv and Tokyo
meanwhile Asia
whose real name is Ariel
or Annabelle or
Abigail
swirls her fruity Stolichnaya
re-crosses her legs and twists
her finely sculpted foot
toenails painted
cherry red
like ten tiny sunsets
my cell vibrating again
eloped to my ass via

my back pocket and
galvanizing my
stupor

sure thing
I'll take that early Mark Tobey
we talked about, and
the Jenny Holzer neon
the David Hockney pastel
the Cindy Sherman selfie
and the Francis Bacon print
the Keith Haring Porsche
if you'll throw in
the Deborah Butterfield
statuette

done deal,
back to the firing squad
as Vinnie always says
camped out in the frozen morning
with his frame and easel
capturing
a street scene enveloped in fog
hitching to Monterey with
stops at sequoia groves
In-N-Out Burger
pumpkin patches
and the bleak majesty of the Pacific
always at his heels
dozing on the beach
at Half Moon Bay

some say he's mad
that he ought to be committed

that he can't be trusted on his own
that painting harasses the dark matter in his head
wearing that crazy hat ringed with candles
sucking down the absinthe
which isn't even made
with wormwood anymore
his pornographic women
and crabbed insistence
on the eternal reward
he'll be the death of me
since I couldn't stand living without him

but it's back to
business
then a bite to eat,
some dim sum at
Yee's on Grant
where guess who struts by
Asia
undoubtably
on her way to catch some Z's
with Vinnie in tow
careening only mildly
happily oblivious to my presence
I watch her ass
the ass of Asia
so enchanting
receding down the sidewalk
Asia
is hotness personified
but in the end
nothing to lose an ear over
still
I'm waiting for the day

Vinnie paints her
to the nose of his F-4 Phantom

the blame

I fell off the teeter-totter
I was kicked out of yoga class
I drank the wrong stuff under the sink

My cat was abducted
My parents were foreigners
My hands couldn't keep to themselves

I threw something through a window
The news the next day read
Terrorist in our midst

I took the bus to Houston
I took the train to Hoboken
I took enough speed to fell a horse

They blamed it
On the imitation
Stratocaster.

bilingual

my dreams
could wallpaper
the Louvre

leah

I miss the names of your children tattooed to your wrists
I miss watching you shoot cocaine into your stomach
I miss vodka orange grapefruit and handcuffs
I miss spanking your wide muscular ass
I miss the holes punched through your bedroom door
I miss Taco Tuesday and you snoring softly
I miss watching football on Sunday in our underwear on speed
I miss cooking eggs for Pierce your son who wanted to play drums in a band
I miss the fact we knew that the next day might be
our last day on earth together
I miss sitting on the barstool next to you smoking and making fun
of our friends
I miss catching you on the toilet with your pants down
doing the last of my coke
I miss your scared drug-addict eyes wheeling about insanely
when I'd get pissed off
I miss your huge tits slopping all over my face as you rode my Jewish cock
I miss you telling total strangers how I make
the best grilled-cheese sandwiches ever
I miss you smiling and laughing about
how nerdy I look when I use my inhaler
I miss how jealous you were of that silly tramp Melissa
I miss hearing about how you whored for old men
out of a sense of pity for them
I miss holding your perfectly proportionate feet
in my grip as I fucked you
I miss the way you'd hide your works from me in the bureau drawer
under your panties
I miss the cab rides where we'd antagonize the driver to no end until he
kicked us out
I miss making out with you a couple of years after we broke up

I miss the utter despair of our union
I miss the fact we were not made for each other
I miss the first day we screwed like an act of desperation
I miss the guns tattooed above your buttocks
I miss teasing you relentlessly until it turned into a fight
I miss your clothes strewn all over the floor

quarantine

running low
on medicine
and source code
for the passage
back
to a simpler
time
we fondly consider
when strapping on
the seat belt

under the bed
or stars
lurk equal
monstrosities

down there amidst
the porn mags and
Hollywood

drawing from life

in the back room of the old shingle factory
they draw furiously
and the model keeps running to the bathroom
to puke
and someone points out how poor the light is
someone else complains that the pose is too rigid
and yet another artiste resents that the model
is constantly running off to puke:
fuckin' junkie!

there in the dusty back room
of the old factory building
where every Thursday night
they draw furiously
as if invoking
the wrecking ball.

not a morning person

I always end up
stuck in some room
with the lights off
pondering the infinite
shades of darkness
cast in a skull.

the ease in which
prone on my back
I ignore the alarm
of simply being
is enough to blind
every bird alive.

daylight slinks
through drab curtains
as I clutch for reasons
to keep up the farce
the utter travail
and insidious yearning.

I always end up
waiting for the bus
on some dirty street
sun and clouds
like the rent
hanging over my head.

it had to be the accent

I don't believe you
or your cats
or your hush-hush Southern upbringing.

you just turned 30
and got a poem published for Metro Poetry on the Buses
you're a redhead by hair-dye
who the hell knows what color your hair
or your soul
really is.

you show up at my place completely hammered
and strip naked
and pull the blinds up so hard they fall out of the window
with a crash!
and then you scream so loud even God
wants to forget he made you.

I mopped up the floor after you spilled red wine
on your skirt and on your shoes
and when you finally passed out it was too late
necrophilia, no thanks.

morning, sweet Princess
you're make-up's all smeared
and there's lipstick on your eye-tooth
I call you a cab.

I don't care if tomorrow is Christmas
or the 4th of July
tonight I save the red wine
from the floor
and from the mop and from you.

shape of a bullet headed home

mom got lung
cancer. girlfriend
sells body
now write a sonnet
kid

when things look bad
hat crushed down
over eyes
asleep slouched in
last seat back of the
bus

how about some
homemade
explosives and the
names of people
responsible. plus
stomach for violence.

sky painted black in
case of pursuit.

the leaders feed
graves with us.
mother and I
wrestle on the
bathroom floor. alert
the media.

war is perpetual. the
animals know it.

let's go camping, she said

my legs, a
landing strip for
mosquitos

face,
a strip mall
for spiders

I shiver
in the obscene
moonlight

eyes like
filmstrip, rattlesnake
theatrics

oh will you quit
whining, she
said

popping me another
beer
as the firelight leapt.

the hermit of the inner sunset

go ahead
just sit there and touch your books
pervert
go ahead fall out of your shoes
fall out the window jump off the Golden Gate
drink bilge and bleach

fondle your volumes like your balls up to your ears
lovingly gaze over the Classics
drunk on a box of wine
it keeps you pickled alive

like vultures stooping to breadcrumbs
like shitty mints in the morgue lobby

like Poe or Baudelaire staring at the crapper walls
go ahead and
just sit there.

north beach black and blue

Hotel living, like paradise, the girl across the hall
She has a nice smile: How are you? her boyfriend's
tattooed up to the neck with Myth
Weird banter on the creaking landing as I pass headed down
the stairs.
I just want to meet one-on-one
a date? Drinks The requisite flirting
maybe playtime Barbary Coast style let's leave the jackals
and werewolves outside
What about the stairwell? there's men dressed in light windbreakers
Khaki shorts running shoes
White socks these men
argue over cigarettes and sports scores while the banisters peel paint
Old sharks hawking phlegm leaning against plate glass out front
the lingerie shop the smoke shop the Tattoo parlor
Latinos play mariachi over distant Eternal radio
The guy with patches of raw skin on his face
across the hall from my room Who pimps the girl
My girl!
He's friendly in a 'don't you dare look at my woman' kind of way,
Plays war simulation video games
At extremely high volume Okay, I can handle depraved modernity
The sultry sodden shower stalls down the hall and
the cockroaches The perpetual incense of hashish fumigating airways
The alarm clock tick-ticking I can deal with
A man immune to ambition.
I walk up Montgomery Street in strange, vibrant November sunlight
A stairway carved from pioneer dishevelment The pinnacle
up near the ceiling of the sky being Coit Tower charged with
Omnipotence
Just below struts Telegraph Hill and mansions most Renaissance

smell the wealth of Heaven in the velveteen air!
I amble about Exclusive as an insect
3 blocks down the hill broken bottles oily street and quantum sleaze
My small room The trafficking of decadence
cage-free ladies leaning and hawkers gesturing with pencil-thin hands,
India ink mustachios Disposable suits and slick foreheads
My address: the Golden Bear the Myriad Parrot the Alley Clown
The glitz and glam of Broadway shunting through the past
Mademoiselle Doda crushed by neon pianissimo
Sailors from the old wars and foreign scent of Beat bookstores
Strident in the night.
Dear Hot Mama across the hall: Where's my deck of Tarot?
I shut my door and converse with baseball legends
Dry out inner band of stingy-brim fedora, the inner Bard
Perched on lampshade with towel and grimace
Genius for the day, dim sum at Yee's
The young Chinese lady suffers my inability to translate coherent thought
instead I smile I pry a smile!
More like a notch of compliance I thank her, ten thousand francs
I eat there a bunch
fortified with cheap sake on the fly, rice and greens, protein
Plus beef soup for just $3.60
They allow a man only a little white plastic fork.
The merchandising of humanity The Babel of Broadway
Yellow tube tiles resounding echoes of tumult
as I take the tunnel through murder of mileage
on first leg headed across the dusk-settled City toward Seal Rock
Great peals of silence and grains of sand ciphering
The vast loneliness

perfect states of innocence

Can't we dim the background
Can't we turn down the soundtrack

My stomach could be the first swimming pool
Scooped out of the moon
But who's racing to patent
Water squeezed from rock

Why are we so lonely
Why are we so unlucky
But most importantly

What happened to that last
Slice of pizza
I was saving for breakfast.

how's it feel to want

I got a baggie over my head
I filled the bathtub full of ketchup
I stole a carp from the Japanese Garden
I smeared my body with avocado
I ate a bottle of Tums

I wiggled and squirmed
I fought and went 'mmphh'
I shook my head 'no no no'
I used a ballpoint to pick the lock
I thrust and parried

I saw a movie once
I paid in francs and yen
I sat directly behind home plate
I beat time with my arm in a cast
I heard a piano falling

I raised an ugly duckling
I squeezed a toothpaste tube
I jumped in wearing handcuffs
I syncopated choking
I gave my heart a hand-job

I sent a text to what's-her-name
I bored a hole in the ceiling
I read up on numerology
I won the fucking lottery
I moved to Lubbock Texas

i liked it better when you were a junkie

your truck was a wreck
your ex-boyfriend camped out on the back porch
the sink filled with dirty dishes
cactus plants dying in the window
feral cats in the yard
vintage cat-eye glasses
crooked on your pretty head.

you liked me because I didn't
cop with you or steal from you
and I always had some weed and enough for a
pint
because I had a job plus
a place to crash.

the only time we slept together
was after your ex-boyfriend threatened
to kill you
your black lab and black eye
between us on the futon.

now
you're married and own a burger joint
your kid is almost 2
you shop at Wal-Mart
Target
and get your contact lenses
at Costco.

your husband sells advertising for an
insurance agency

and after your dad died
you could afford that house in Auburn Hills.

I haven't heard from you in over a
year
which is the natural progression
of things
when you grow up and get
a life.

call me romantic
but I liked it better when you were a junkie.

the legacy

try to delete hangover
with pages from encyclopedia in blender
add smelling salts
solar sludge
cumin, lime
wedge of arrogance
succumb against brick wall like crash test dummy
laurels smoking over skull
eyeholes infinite
ballet slipper stuffed in jawbone

hollywood

A little smoke
After a meal
Watch a movie
Seal it

We kissed and the moon
Closer to the earth than ever
Shone on the wall
Of the living room

Death forgotten
The songs of the nightingale
Who won at backgammon
Catastrophe overseas

Up the stairs
Through fumbling dark
Giggling stupidly
I'll shave in the morning

New to darling
Aghast at longing
Goodnight one hour
Exhausted at last

Following the moon
Closer to home
Than ever before
Imminent disaster

the short term

after a small and inconsequential misunderstanding
she gives me a chance to redeem myself, to utter some untruth,
to assuage her skinned-knee pride.

I roll over, say
forget it, just go.
I've had it with you.

your behavior is barbaric
and you ought to live in a cave
that's what she tells me
swallowing the last of the wine,
clomping around in her shoes.
on her way out she slams the door.

if only I could fake how I don't feel
she'd still be here,
boring me to tears.

no hand in the naming

he wakes me in the morning
same as he pumped my mother full of life
with brazen alacrity
the old Caddy's motor running
'Let's take a ride, son!'
gun down South Jackson
swing up 2nd uptown
his polished white wingtips working the pedals
scattering flocks of pigeons
side by side front seat of a
canary yellow 1972 Eldorado
'Still runs like a top!'
strange twins forged from insidious ores
father whose literacy treads
stock options and box scores
father who had no hand in the naming
of a child begotten faceless and
murder to raise
'Say Pop? Ever picture Mom's face
while you were screwing all those shore-leave whores
back in Korea?'
'Gotta spread the wealth, son!'
pull into a Chevron Full Serve
DING-DING!
'Fill 'er up! 'N check the oil, willya?'
at full speed back out on the highway
I look the old man in the eye
open the door whoosh to the wind
and throw my body to the coyotes

fish

Hell is rough on fish
I dive in the shallow end of the pool
Swim for my life in desperate attempt
To recover my eyes like out of my face fallen dice
Lungs clogged from oil spill refugee of the Ark
I fall in with a dark crowd, last of the species
Doomed from the get-go, peering up umbilical periscope
Eyeing a lure the sure shape of the sun
Rise through the shadowy silence like a real fish
While carved from diamond the gleam of the hook entices
Hell
Is hard enough, and then you're caught
Say you're a fish.

a moment of introspection

I love my flannel green
bicycle, Peugeot single-speed
Swiss knives, my pot and pan
the Uni-Ball pen
morning gulp of cold clean water
comics and sports page
an old Impala say 1963
my brothers
baseball
Jolly Ranchers
a good scratch
the polished pool cue
old leather shoes
and my specs
in order to see
what I
love
all too
well
and all too
fleetingly.

hotel modigliani

That's right, Dedo,
I'm holed up in sketch.
#208 boards a hostile beauty
I see her sometimes in the hallway.

Outside,
the rain elucidates upon
how to wipe out the town, and recon
with the flu.

the night bores through the walls
causing the TV screen to flicker
and spark.

Okay, Dedo, I kept that photo of Jeanne H.
tacked to the wall
next to the shuddering fridge
when I could've easily
heralded it for a shot of
murky absinthe.

The door hinge to my little fetid room
needs a good dose of
WD-40.

All night down the hall, sick
of porcelain and the whispering of roaches-
I can't keep anything down or
rooted.

I forget how to test the mattress

for real. Or how to
piss in the sink like a man.

Eyeless, or mere slits
sultry Jeanne from the pic
stares at the same walls.

Dedo. I got a flu that flows like
the ancient rivers
of Mars.

Sometimes I forget
where I am. When I see shapes
without contours. When trucks
growl past the window, slashing
through the dirty rain.

Girlfriend in #208's
half my age, yet twice as wise.
She scowls in the hallway.

I've finished painting
for the day.

shell shock

You fell out of the sky
And leveled the city
The night I had tickets
To play the ponies

Why you always gotta turn the mountain
To silicon on days I'm feeling lucky
Coat just back from the cleaners
Wing-tips spit-shined

Rubble and smoking ruin
Phosphorous, sinister calm
I gotta hand it to you
You busted up my trifecta

Temple gates fallen to dust
Flames a mile high
And you haven't even
Put on your make-up

romance

embattled we meet
make rain between us

at knifepoint
slit belly of sky blue

rain like wine, red wine, blood red
we rend apart the world

never to arrive
again as one

at once
at war

blackjack

there's the baseball game
on scratchy AM radio
4 floors up
elevator shaky
after picking through the scattered remains
of the Tenderloin
maneuvering around
turds on the street
and burst bags of garbage
the huddled sunken leathery drunks
piercing sunlight without respite
windowglass scorched, graffitied
the cars go by while the clientele
of the nouveau cafes and boutiques
are
smoothly oblivious
there's crackheads
pirouetting into traffic off Sutter
and as dusk descends and the
bar crowd surges
the trannies post gargantuan mammaries and
butcher-knife high stilettos
on the corners and mouths of alleys
gloriously painted and preening
it's a certain aroma
sighs on optimum and
eyes on the prize
advancing
step by step through the debris
the souped-up trucks, beneath police radar, rolling 24/7
the Latino boys on the corners

or are they Hispanic
they got what you need
so you
roll with it
bliss factor introverted with brewing violence
it's when shit gets scary
and sirens start in from the pavement up
to hammer the sky with fireworks
the depth of the night
at the heart of it all
drawing us in
beckoning us
with a wry smile
with blackjack force
with unnerving connivance
back
back to where we belong

the gospel according to acid pete

I felt like a cat
on a treadmill
chasing a can
of tuna.

I was sitting at the bar
at the Wing Nut
next to
her and Woody.

she dangled a pinky
in her vodka
orange
and smiled at me.

use your inhaler again,
she said,
let me try on your
glasses.

I complied. she looked like
a streetwalker
in a library
as I shot
albuterol
into my wheeze and chased it
with Monte Alban.

ooh, eat the
worm,
she giggled.

yeah Jay, eat the worm,
said deadpan Woody.

dream on, Woody, she laughed, you
only wish. I think he's
cute.

I got up and shot some pool. I took Acid Pete
for 5 bucks, which I put into the
juke. for 5 bucks I got
5 songs.

that new juke
is a fucking rip off, observed
Acid Pete.
I stood waiting for Pete
to rack 'em up.

why do you always play
Velvet Underground
songs?

their sound is still
relevant, I said, looking over
to make sure she was watching
me.

Lou Reed sang about
waiting to score
while I shot
another game of 9 ball with
Acid Pete.

Woody ordered us all

a pitcher. Woody worked
at the concrete
foundry and took hydrocodone
for his bad
back.

why don't you come up
to the Ranch later,
Woody asked,
winking like a barnyard
owl.

the Ranch was what
Woody called
the house in Lower Phinney
that he shared
with Leah and Acid Pete.

Leah was in the
lady's room
dabbing at her wide Scandinavian features
after
doing a fat
line off the toilet tank.

she likes you,
said Woody,
as I sank the 6 off a side
bank.

you might as well just put
the 5 into the juke,
Pete, I said.

hardy har, said Acid Pete.

feel sick and dirty
more dead than alive,
sang Lou.

on the couch at the Ranch
I was down to boxer
shorts and
felt her hands crawling up my
back
like the tiny white mice you feed to snakes.

Woody was passed out on the
recliner. the TV was on
Comedy Central and Leah's
tits were pressed up
against me.
take off your glasses, she
panted, take off your
boxers.

why don't we
party in your
room?

Leah looked confused for
a second. she was
wasted. I pulled her up off the couch
and she crookedly
led me down
the hall.

the door to her bedroom

had a bunch
of holes punched through
it.

that was Woody, she said.

I guess he likes to use his fists, I
replied.

you don't know the half of it.

in the morning I noticed Leah's
hands were quite shapely and
proportionate.
she snored quietly
as
the blinds let in some weak
light.

I got up and raided the fridge
for some beers.
I was pulling the Stoli bottle
from the freezer
when Acid Pete
appeared. Acid Pete
was so skinny, he looked like chopsticks with
eyes.

that's Woody's vodka, he said.

don't worry, I said, I won't
tell him
you drank any.

Acid Pete cracked a beer and
looked at me. you know I used
to date Leah? and
before I dated her, Woody
dated her.

she sounds pretty dated, I said.

you don't mind?

I poured some Stoli
into a glass. nah, I don't mind,
I said. but from now on, she's gonna
cost you.

Acid Pete relaxed
a little, chuckling. yeah,
that's what Woody
said.

how much did he
charge?

Acid Pete cracked another beer and
lit a smoke. it was 8
in the
morning.

he took it off my rent,
said Acid Pete.

they may very well turn against me

my feet would
burst
living this
long

music derived
from the center of
nocturnal ambience

I mock dance, minions of
death

this is not especially
modern.
my friends are
going to be very angry.

they may very
well turn
against me.

I hate my feet
and the unfeeling dance
the desire of
music

bursting into
flowers
the soil
enamors, insect life

the beatitude would expire
at the typewritten song

as it does
every day
easy as butter
melting in the sky

as if
through fog

say a city
say a snake

anything
hungry
anything angry
enough

to mention.

how to go hungry when revoked of dreams

to steep our need
in relentlessness.

it used to be we could
count on

trains
factories
roosters in the cold a.m.
cheap cans of beer and stolen chocolate
rainy day reasons
to pout and blather
cold roast beef
on stale rye bread
savoring the blood terrain
of bolt-action murder.

we used to count on
pinball
the pennant race
punk rock driven hard with a
snarl
talking up a healthy milkmaid
in the dark part of the lounge
to the rear

we used to be seers.

modern art

Pain not paint
mother not a
madman
Say there
Dad
how is it I made an artist
from thrown clay
stones and bones
bombed out cities
Stroke of luck
Downright genius
armed with a chisel
appropriating a young woman with guilt
Art is short for Artillery
Tanks of Industrial Origin
2 dogs riding
a horse
in 1932 on the blue hills
deep in Russian
territory.

my way

the old man and I
didn't get along all that well
at the time

1980
the year I turned 15
my older sister was living on a kibbutz in Israel

she had a blue Datsun 200-SX
which sat out front of the house
practically abandoned

my old man smoked weed
I used to go through his bathroom drawers
because that's where he stashed it

one day I noticed
the set of keys
to the Datsun

I played around with the idea for about a week
and since the old man never broached the subject
I decided to educate myself

at first it was just a spin
around the block
nothing serious

then one day my pal Eddie was over after school
so we went for a quick beer run
which meant waiting at the corner store

for some kind soul over 21
to buy up for us
then back into the Datsun

we drove over to Teri's and Gloria's
picked 'em up and headed to The Shells
which was a little beach near the San Mateo Bridge

nothing serious
just some beers and cigarettes and weed
at the ass end of San Francisco Bay

the old man always came home late
the car safely back in place
me in my room high as a kite

buzzing with hormones and chemicals
listening to the Steve Miller Band
or Zeppelin

eventually came a weekend when
the old man was out of town
for the weekend on business

Eddie and Teri and Gloria and I
took the Datsun all the way to San Francisco
which was about a 40 mile jaunt

at Haight Street we scored
some LSD
and hit Golden Gate Park

it was a sunshine spectacular

Eddie took a photo of me strumming a guitar
sitting indian-style under a tree

when I turned 16 the old man
drove us in his Caddy to some empty parking lot
where I went through the motions

for about 15 minutes
he was a bit suspicious that I seemed to know what I was doing
which made me nervous

I barely passed the driving test
since I didn't know the rule for when to take a left turn
when faced with oncoming traffic

almost getting the instructor
and myself killed in a very close call
he glared at me and said

I shouldn't pass you
but I suppose
you'll never forget that rule again

for the old man's birthday
the following January
I had the picture from Golden Gate Park framed

that's a good picture of you
he said
then he hung it up in his bathroom.

war

there's news
from the trees

crows report
meds in short

supply at the
front

I reach for the
remote

nowadays

Waltzing to placebos of time clocks
Menace of lip and beard.

Sparrows hopping on the wet green grass
Holes in my socks and shoes.

It doesn't pay to think
Thought, plus tax.

The romantic man climbs the roof to embrace the sun
Holds it close to scorch and kiss.

Sparrows pecking at the wet green grass
Luring tomcats.

All I know about politics is
I'm always broke.

history

it gave off the delicate stench
of carrion
vultures descended from moon shafts
men rounded the fields in search of bone filament
to seat their weapons anew
roan bulls grazed the new shoots
beneath the descent of ghastly reconnaissance
how many hundreds of years ago?
Beethoven
had yet to brandish ear trumpet
Spain
busy minting the currency of Inquisition
in the creek-bed of the homestead
stood quicksilver reflectivity spanning the shaman gleam
from wizardry to digitization
I wandered
into the disheveled earshot of a girl
I cooed
'tell me a secret'

middle east of complacency

because there are rules and the hands must obey the rules
something to flush down and
make boom
a Pineapple
a Pomegranate
because the destruction is palpable and intuitive
war crimes Sterilization of God blackened maize of minefields
because death of love is a symphony
because life is like a stake shoved into the earth
The deflowering of a national vampire
a Poem in celebration of
sandbags and flugelhorn
because I could carve a turkey out of Time
stink like a camel
ride straight into Armageddon
make room
go boom

old men clutching

old men clutching transistor radios glued to elephant ears
cream white Schwinn bicycle
photographs bordered and yellowing
body more of an exclamation point or less of an apostrophe
a baseball between the ears
bicarbonate of nowhere near and hardly heard
skipping stones flat over the cold stream
birds
and old men
and radio programs
and tape recorders
the satisfaction of a hit song recorded quite primitively
the air a song of photographic memory
a home made meal out of a can
the first microwave
every man wearing a fedora
every woman with a slip beneath
saccharine for the coffee cup
wars declared
books condemned
and old men
and newsprint
loose on the fingertips
and domestic factories teeming with strife
paintings of lovers and angels and fauna
terrifying gods
and saturday morning cartoons
a lunch box
being told to quit sulking and go play outside
the sunshine a normalcy of utter crescendo
the first
skateboard

tobacco rolled with rice paper
a box of matches advertising an auto repair shop
bright candid coloring crayons
Sunday morning delicatessen spread
old men
muttering at formica tables
cigars and coffee in chipped ceramic cups
a pain between the knees

power out(r)age

living in the hotel
it's not like gay Paree
or Constantinople in the 20s
except for when the lights go out
not like being bombed
shellacked from the sky
critters scurrying
in any case
they got a bicycle connected to the generator
to fork out the headlines
along with the morning Nescafe
well
it's not like that
these are modern times verging on real live
Futurism
I just get pissed off
grab the cell phone
turn on the flashlight app and commence
to put the finishing touches on my manifesto on how to burn it
all down
and when
and why
instructions via hot-wired literati
it's not like I need a candle
I'm not taking a bath
nobody fucking died

missy

Missy stole my camera
to pawn for junk
I can't blame her
I let her sleep over
but nothing happened
Missy being a lesbian
Missy sleeps on her back
and snores
I sleep on the floor
through the open window
second hand smoke and
black night stalling
cool apocalypse
I let her go with her acne
slanted eye and feline slouch
her So-Cal gutter accent
she relieved me of
2 pairs of boxer shorts as well
after I lent her my soap
so she could take a shower
Missy was very excited
Your soap's so minty!
she exclaimed
as if she were 5 years old
I got this soft spot for junkies

Grateful acknowledgment to the editors of the following publications where many of these poems first appeared: *2014 Friends of the San Francisco Public Library Poets 11 Anthology, 2016 High Window Press Four American Poets Anthology, 2017 Pski's Porch's Resurrection of a Sunflower Anthology, 3 AM Magazine, 3rd Wednesday, ALBA, Alternative Reel, Black-Listed Magazine, Caliban, Camel Saloon, Clutching at Straws, Dead Snakes, Deuce Coupe, Drunken Absurdity, Graffiti Kolkata, Grandma Moses Press, Guerrilla Pamphlets, Haggard & Halloo, Horror Sleaze Trash, Instant Pussy, Kmart Fashion, Mad Rush, Mad Swirl, Media Virus, Night Ballet, Nothing but the Truth, Odd Magazine, Orion Headless, Pigeon Bike, Poetry Super Highway, Ppigpenn, Really Earnest, Red Fez, Right Hand Pointing, Silver Birch Press, Small Doggies, Unlikely Stories Mark V, Why Vandalism?, Your One Phone Call*

Pski's Porch Publishing was formed July 2012, to make books for people who like people who like books. We hope we have some small successes.
www.pskisporch.com.

Pski's Porch
323 East Avenue
Lockport, NY 14094
www.pskisporch.com

www.ingramcontent.com/pod-product-compliance
Lightning Source LLC
Chambersburg PA
CBHW060332050426
42449CB00011B/2739